really easy piano

QUEEN

ISBN: 978-1-5400-4811-0

For all works contained herein:
Unauthorized copying, arranging, adapting, recording, Internet posting, public performance, or other distribution of the music in this publication is an infringement of copyright. Infringers are liable under the law.

Visit Hal Leonard Online at
www.halleonard.com

Contact us:
Hal Leonard
7777 West Bluemound Road
Milwaukee, WI 53213
Email: info@halleonard.com

In Europe, contact:
Hal Leonard Europe Limited
42 Wigmore Street
Marylebone, London, W1U 2RY
Email: info@halleonardeurope.com

In Australia, contact:
Hal Leonard Australia Pty. Ltd.
4 Lentara Court
Cheltenham, Victoria, 3192 Australia
Email: info@halleonard.com.au

QUEEN

QUEEN

Another One Bites The Dust 6
Bohemian Rhapsody 9
Breakthru 12
Crazy Little Thing Called Love 15
Don't Stop Me Now 18
I Want It All 21
I Want To Break Free 24
Killer Queen 27
A Kind Of Magic 30
Radio Ga Ga 32
Save Me 35
Seven Seas Of Rhye 38
The Show Must Go On 41
Somebody To Love 44
Too Much Love Will Kill You 47
Under Pressure 50
We Are The Champions 56
We Will Rock You 58
Who Wants To Live Forever 53
You're My Best Friend 60

Another One Bites The Dust

Words & Music by John Deacon

This single from Queen was written by bass player, John Deacon, and released in 1980 as part of their album of the same year, *The Game*. A nod to the disco style is apparent in this track, as Deacon explains how he was influenced by Chic's single, 'Good Times'. Originally, the band did not consider releasing it as a single until music mogul Michael Jackson convinced them to do just that!

Hints & Tips: Practice the syncopation in the chorus a few times so you grasp the rhythm. The left-hand sixteenth note should sound at exactly the same time as the right-hand sixteenth note.

Copyright © 1980 Queen Music Ltd.
All Rights Administered by Sony/ATV Music Publishing LLC, 424 Church Street, Suite 1200, Nashville, TN 37219
International Copyright Secured All Rights Reserved

10
C
G
C
G
hang-ing on the edge of your seat?
Out of the door - way the bul - lets rip
12
Am
B
Em
to the sound of the beat.
An -
14
Am
Em
-oth - er one bites the dust.
An -
16
Am
Em
-oth - er one bites the dust.
And an -
oth - er one gone, and an - oth - er one gone.
An -
18
Am
F♯m
-oth - er one bites the dust.
Hey!
I'm gon - na get you too.
An -

20
B
Em
-oth - er one bites the dust.
22
Am
Em
24
Am
C
G
26
C
G
C
G
28
Am
B
Em

Bohemian Rhapsody

Words & Music by Freddie Mercury

The first song ever to reach to No. 1 twice with the same version, winner of just about every musical award there is, and one of only two contemporary tracks to make it into the UK's Desert Island Discs Top 8, this internationally-acclaimed work of genius can justifiably claim to be the most revered six minutes in the history of rock music.

Hints & Tips: Note the time signature changes at the beginning.
Bring out the harmonies at the start as they play a big part in the feel of the song.
Play through the passages with accidentals thoroughly as some of these are quite tricky.

Fairly free tempo ♩ = 72

Gm7 G7

Is this the real life? Is this just fan - ta - sy?

mp

3 F7 B♭ F7 B♭

Caught in a land - slide, no es - cape from re - al - i - ty.

5 Gm B♭7

O - pen your eyes, look up to the skies and

7 E♭ Cm F7

see. I'm just a poor boy, I need no sym - path - y 'cause I'm

Copyright © 1975 Queen Music Ltd.
Copyright Renewed
All Rights Administered by Sony/ATV Music Publishing LLC, 424 Church Street, Suite 1200, Nashville, TN 37219
International Copyright Secured All Rights Reserved

10
N.C.
eas - y come, eas - y go, lit - tle high, lit - tle low,
12
E♭
B♭/D
C♯dim
F7/C
An - y way the wind blows, does - n't real - ly mat - ter to
14
B♭
me, to me.
mf
17
B♭
Gm
Cm
Ma - ma, just killed a man, put a gun a - gainst his head, pulled my
20
F7
B♭
Gm
trig - ger, now he's dead. Ma - ma, life had just be - gun but

23
Cm
Am7♭5
A♭
E♭/G
E♭
B♭
now I've gone and thrown it all a - way.
Ma - ma, ooh,
f
26
Cm
Fm
B♭
did - n't mean to make you cry, if I'm not back a - gain this time to -
29
E♭
B♭/D
Cm
A♭m
E♭
-mor - row, car - ry on, car - ry on, as if noth - ing real - ly mat - ters.
32
Cm
Gm
Cm
Gm
Cm
A♭m
Noth - ing real - ly mat - ters, an - y - one can see, noth - ing real - ly mat - ters,
mp
35
E♭/B♭
B♭sus4
B♭
E♭
noth - ing real - ly mat - ters to me.

Breakthru

Words & Music by Freddie Mercury, Brian May, Roger Taylor and John Deacon

The rapid rhythmic beat of this song is strongly reminiscent of a steam train thundering along the tracks. So, in the video that accompanied its release as a single, shot on the Nene Valley Railway near Cambridge, the band perform onboard an old locomotive, renamed The Miracle Express.

Hints & Tips: Keep the driving quarter notes going steadily throughout to maintain the pace.

Copyright © 1989 Queen Music Ltd.
All Rights Administered by Sony/ATV Music Publishing LLC, 424 Church Street, Suite 1200, Nashville, TN 37219
International Copyright Secured All Rights Reserved

16
B♭
Dm
E♭
C7
I'm un - der your thumb, un - der your spell, can't you see?
20
F
C
If I could on - ly reach you, if I could make you smile.
24
B♭
If I could on - ly reach you, that would real - ly be a
28
F
N.C.
break - thru. Oh, yeah.
32
F
E♭/F
Break - thru these bar - ri - ers of pain.
f

36
F
E♭/F
Break - thru, yeah, in - to the sun - shine from the rain,
40
Dm
G
make my feel - ings known to - wards you, turn my heart in - side and out for
44
F/A
B♭
you now.
Some-how I have to make this
48
Dm
Am/C
B♭
Gm/C
fi - nal break - thru.
52
F
Now!

Crazy Little Thing Called Love

Words & Music by Freddie Mercury

Allegedly composed by Freddie Mercury whilst having a bath, in 1980 it became Queen's first No. 1 single in the USA. *The Game*, the album on which it featured, was the first Queen album to be released on CD, their first to reach No. 1 in the US and the first to use synthesizers, as the band adopted the bass-driven grooves of the day.

Hints & Tips: Keep both hands light throughout. Look through the piece carefully before playing to make sure you know where all the accidentals are. Count through bars 33–36, making sure full value is given to the rests in between the triplets.

Copyright © 1979 Queen Music Ltd.
All Rights Administered by Sony/ATV Music Publishing LLC, 424 Church Street, Suite 1200, Nashville, TN 37219
International Copyright Secured All Rights Reserved

13
D
G
thing called love it cries in a
16
C
G
D
cra - dle all night, it swings, it jives, it
19
G
C
G
D
shakes all o - ver like a jel - ly fish. I kind - a like it.
22
B♭
C
D
Cra - zy lit - tle thing called love. There goes my
25
G
C
ba - by, she knows how to rock 'n' roll.

28
G
B♭
She drives me cra - zy, she gives me
31
E
A
F
hot and cold fe - ver, then she leaves me in a cool, cool sweat.
33
N.C.
35
E7
A7
D.S. al Coda
This
Coda
37
D
B♭
C
D
love.
Cra - zy lit - tle thing called love.

Don't Stop Me Now

Words & Music by Freddie Mercury

The first Queen single released on a cassette tape, this song has become one of the most frequently covered. A version by McFly, which was the official song for *Sport Relief 2006*, reached No. 1 in the UK Singles Chart in July, a year after being voted 'The Greatest Driving Song Ever' by viewers of the BBC TV programme *Top Gear*.

Hints & Tips: This song is quite fast, so start off by practicing it slowly and build up speed once you're more confident. There are some big stretches in the melody, so take the time to look at the fingering.

Copyright © 1978 Queen Music Ltd.
All Rights Administered by Sony/ATV Music Publishing LLC, 424 Church Street, Suite 1200, Nashville, TN 37219
International Copyright Secured All Rights Reserved

12
F/E♭
B♭/D
burn - ing through the sky, yeah, two
14
Gm/B♭
D7
hun - dred de - grees that's why they call me Mis - ter Fah - ren -
16
Gm
D7
Gm
- heit. I'm trav - 'ling at the speed of light, I wan - na make a
19
G/B
C7
F
Gm
Am
Dm
su - per - son - ic man out - ta you.
Don't stop me now,
22
Gm/B♭
C7
I'm hav - ing such a good time, I'm hav - ing a ball.

25
F Gm Am Dm F Gm Am Dm
Don't stop me now, if you wan - na have a
27
Gm/B♭ D7 Gm F Gm/B♭
good time, just give me a call. Don't stop me, 'cause I'm
30
Gm F Gm/B♭
hav - ing a good time, don't stop, yes I'm
32
Gm C7 1. F
hav - ing a good time, I don't wan - na stop at all. I'm
2. B♭ rit. B♭m7 F
35
all.

I Want It All

Words & Music by Freddie Mercury, Brian May, Roger Taylor and John Deacon

Despite songwriter Brian May claiming that it is merely about having ambitions and fighting for one's own goals, featuring themes of rebellion and social upheaval, this heavy rock number from *The Miracle*, Queen's sixth UK No. 1 album, became an anti-apartheid song in South Africa and a rallying anthem for African-American youth.

Hints & Tips: The melody in the right hand has a few leaps; be aware of where these are and make sure your hand is in the correct position.

Copyright © 1989 Queen Music Ltd.
All Rights Administered by Sony/ATV Music Publishing LLC, 424 Church Street, Suite 1200, Nashville, TN 37219
International Copyright Secured All Rights Reserved

11
A
G
A
1
fu - ture, move out of my way. I want it
13
Bm
G
A
all, I want it all, I want it all, and I want it
16
Bm
A
Bm
G
To Coda
now. I want it all, I want it all, I want it
19
A
Bm
G
all, and I want it now. List - en all you
21
Bm
5
G
peo - ple, come gath - er round. I got - ta get me a

23
A
Bm
A
game plan, got - ta shake you to the ground. Just
25
Bm
G
A
give me, what I know is mine, peo-ple do you hear me? Just
28
Bm
A
D
G
give me the sign. It ain't much I'm ask - ing, if you want the
D.S. al Coda
30
A
G
A
truth, here's to the fu - ture for the dreams of youth. I want it
Coda
33
A
B
all. And I want it now.

I Want To Break Free

Words & Music by John Deacon

Written in 1983 by bassist John Deacon and influenced by prevailing men's attitudes to the women's liberation movement, this song came to be regarded as an anthem for the fight against oppression. Its original music video featured the band dressed in women's clothes in a parody of the long-running soap, *Coronation Street*.

Hints & Tips: There are a lot of triplets in this song, so take care they are not rushed and make them nice and even.

Copyright © 1984 Queen Music Ltd.
All Rights Administered by Sony/ATV Music Publishing LLC, 424 Church Street, Suite 1200, Nashville, TN 37219
International Copyright Secured All Rights Reserved

12
G
D
N.C.
God knows I want to break free.
I've fall - en in
15
D
love,
I've fall - en in
love for the first time and
18
G
this time I know it's for
real.
I've fall - en in
21
D
A
love.
Yeah.
God
knows,
24
G
D
God knows I've fall - en in
love.
It's

27
A
G
A
strange but it's true, hey, I can't get o - ver the way you
30
G
Bm7
love me like you do, but I have to be sure when I
32
walk out that door. Oh, how I want to be
34
G
A
free, ba - by, oh, how I want to be
36
Bm
G
A
D
free, oh, how I want to be free.

Killer Queen

Words & Music by Freddie Mercury

As disclosed by Freddie Mercury, this song is about 'a high class call girl'. From their 1974 album, *Sheer Heart Attack*, this track was Queen's first major breakthrough into the worldwide singles charts. The most famous line from the song is, 'let them eat cake, she says, just like Marie Antoinette', as it refers to the legend that Marie Antoinette — the last Queen of France before the French Revolution — made this insensitive remark upon hearing that the peasants had no bread to eat.

Hints & Tips: Take care over the changes of time signature throughout this song. Practice these passages several times to get a hang of them, using a metronome and counting out the quarter notes if useful.

Copyright © 1974 Queen Music Ltd.
Copyright Renewed
All Rights Administered by Sony/ATV Music Publishing LLC, 424 Church Street, Suite 1200, Nashville, TN 37219
International Copyright Secured All Rights Reserved

9
A/C♯
Dm
Cav - i - ar and cig - a - rettes,
11
C
F
E
Am
G/B
well versed in et - i - quette, ex - tr'or - di - nar - i - ly nice. She's a
13
C
Em
Am
Em
kill - er queen, gun - pow - der, gel - a - tine,
15
Am
B7
Em
A
dy - na - mite with a la - ser beam, guar - an - teed to blow your

17
D
C
B7
Em
mind,
an - y time, ooh.
Re - com - mend - ed at the price, in -

20
A7
Dm
C
sat - tia - ble an ap - pe - tite,
what a drag.

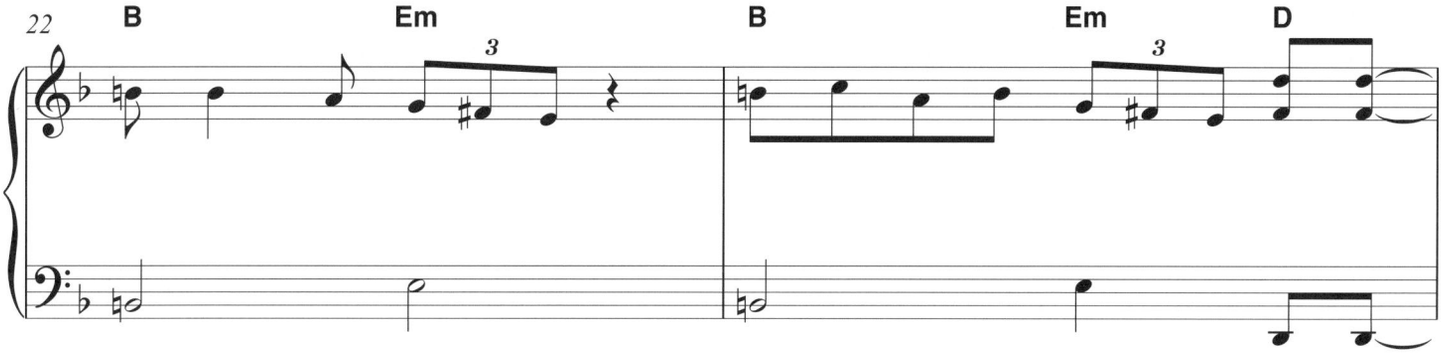
22
B
Em
B
Em
D

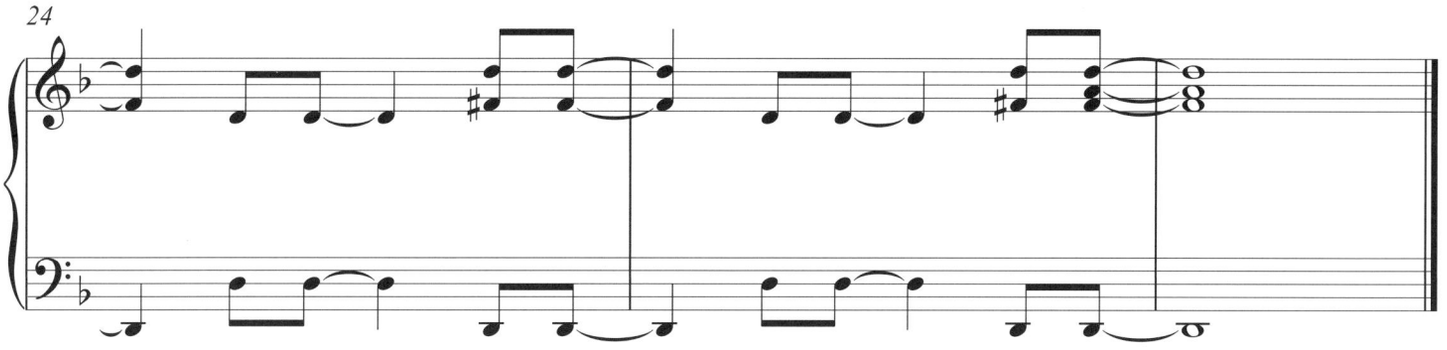
24

A Kind Of Magic

Words & Music by Roger Taylor

On the basis of their strong, anthemic songs, in 1985 Queen were commissioned to compose music for the soundtrack of the movie *Highlander*. This project expanded into their 12th studio album *A Kind Of Magic*, which includes this song by Roger Taylor, the lyrics of which make several references to snippets from the film's script.

Hints & Tips: Keep the left hand at a constant and steady beat throughout. Don't let this overpower the melody, but bring it out whenever the left hand has the eighth-note patterns which mimic the tune.

Copyright © 1986 Queen Music Ltd.
All Rights Administered by Sony/ATV Music Publishing LLC, 424 Church Street, Suite 1200, Nashville, TN 37219
International Copyright Secured All Rights Reserved

15
2.
G
A
The bell that rings in - side your mind, is
20
C
G
Em
chal - leng-ing the doors of time. The wait - ing
25
C
Em
seems e - ter - ni - ty, the day will dawn of
30
D
C
G
sa - ni - ty. Is this a kind of ma-gic?
35
Slower
C
G

Radio Ga Ga

Words & Music by Roger Taylor

Written by Queen's drummer, Roger Taylor, this song was inspired by a comment made by his infant son on hearing something which he didn't like on the radio. The lyrics reference two important radio events; a 1938 broadcast by Orson Welles and Winston Churchill's 'This was their finest hour' wartime speech from June 1940.

Hints & Tips: Keep the beat strong and steady in this one and be wary of accidentals.

Copyright © 1983 Queen Music Ltd.
All Rights Administered by Sony/ATV Music Publishing LLC, 424 Church Street, Suite 1200, Nashville, TN 37219
International Copyright Secured All Rights Reserved

2.
10
Fsus4
F
So don't be - come some back - ground noise, a
13
Fm/A♭
B♭
G7/B♭
back - drop for the girls and boys who just don't know, or
16
G7/B
just don't care, and just com - plain when you're not there. You
19
F/A
C7
had your time you had the power, you've yet to have your
22
B♭
F
B♭
F
fi - nest hour. Ra - di - o.

25
F/E♭
B♭
F
B♭
F
All we hear___ is
Ra - di - o Ga Ga,
Ra - di - o Goo - goo,
28
B♭
F
F/E♭
B♭
F
Ra - di - o Ga Ga.
All we hear___ is
Ra - di - o Ga Ga
31
B♭
F
E♭
B♭
C
Ra - di - o Bla - bla.
Ra - di - o_____ what's new?___
34
Dm
F/C
C
Csus4
C
Ra - di - o,_____
some - one
still loves
37
F
you!_____

Save Me

Words & Music by Brian May

This rock ballad was written by Queen's virtuoso guitarist, Brian May, about a friend whose relationship had ended. In recent years May returned to post-graduate studies in astrophysics, for which he was awarded a PhD by Imperial College, London in 2008, completion of his thesis coming 30 years after he started his research.

Hints & Tips: Starting off softly and slowly, this song changes key for a contrasting chorus, which should be played louder. Bars 23 & 28 should be played through slowly to make sure you've got the hang of the rhythm, fingering and accidentals.

Copyright © 1980 Queen Music Ltd.
All Rights Administered by Sony/ATV Music Publishing LLC, 424 Church Street, Suite 1200, Nashville, TN 37219
International Copyright Secured All Rights Reserved

10
C
Am/C
G
loy - al - ty were noth - ing but a sham, it
ad - ver - tise a soul for sale or

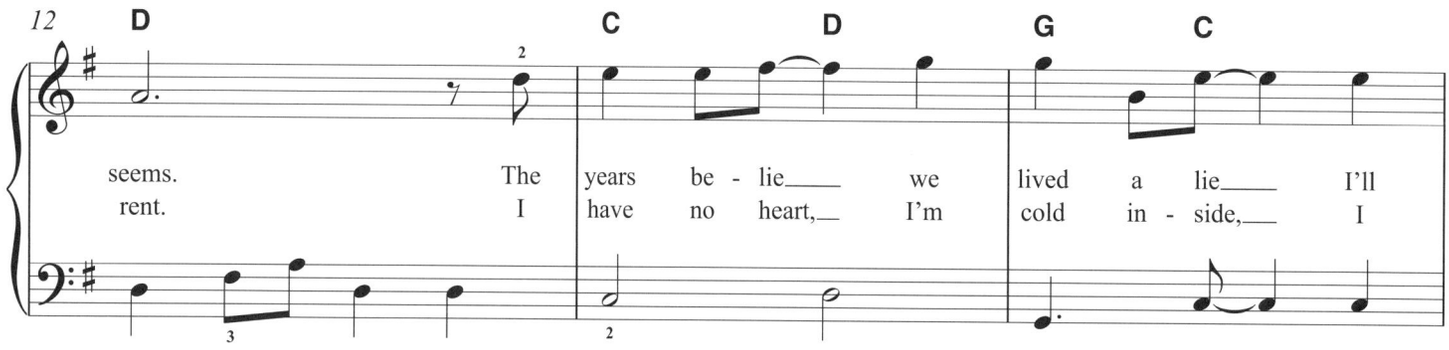
12
D
C
D
G
C
seems. The years be - lie we lived a lie I'll
rent. I have no heart, I'm cold in - side, I

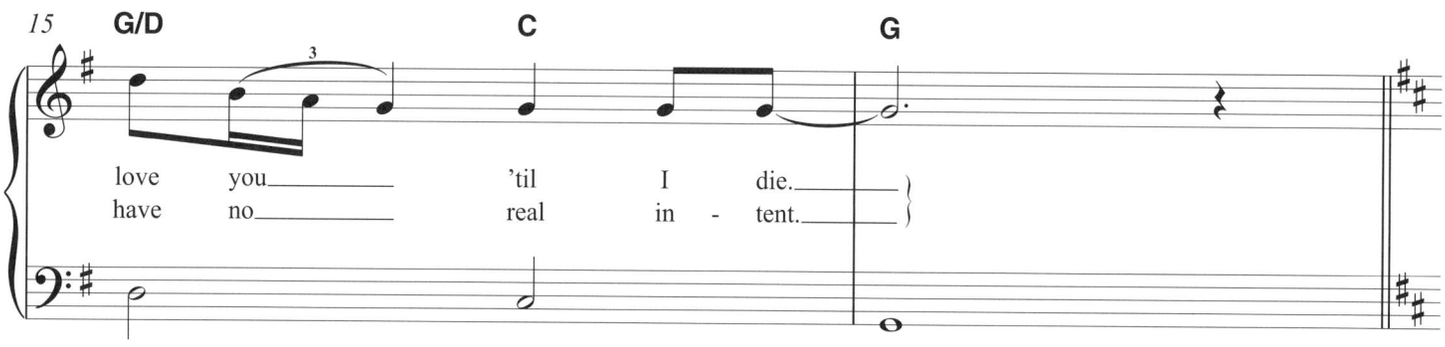
15
G/D
C
G
love you 'til I die.
have no real in - tent.

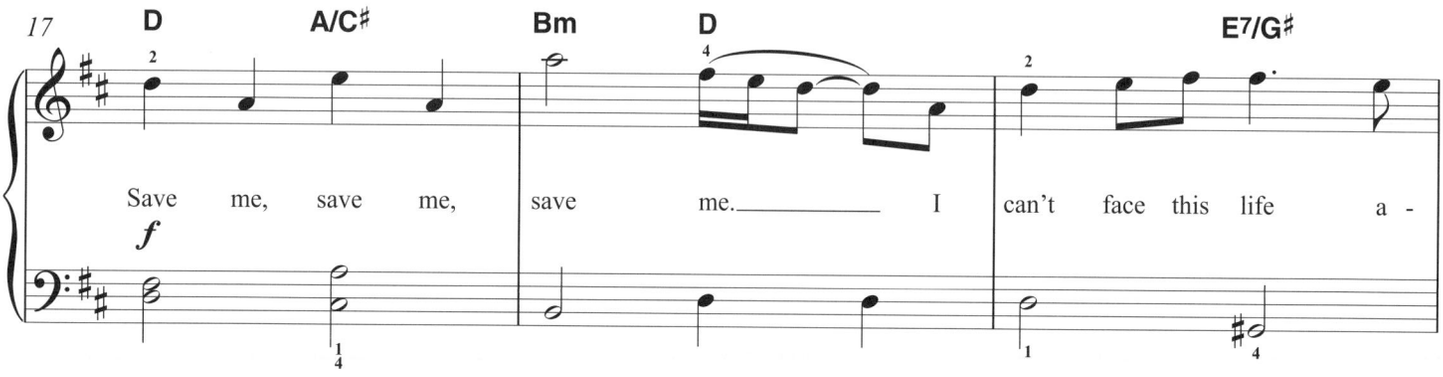
17
D
A/C♯
Bm
D
E7/G♯
Save me, save me, save me. I can't face this life a -
f

20
A G D A/C♯ D/C G/B Gm/B♭
- lone
Save me, save me,
save me. I'm

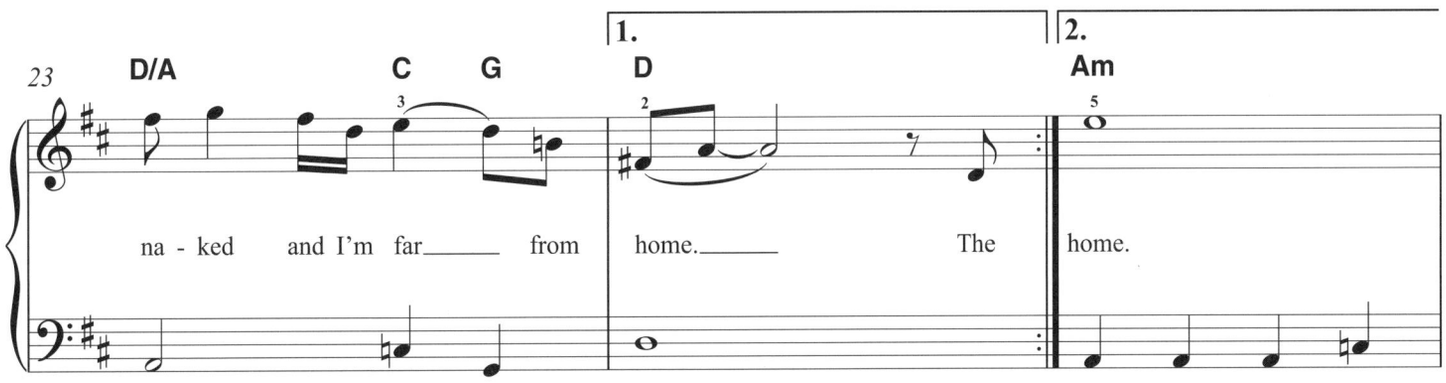
23
D/A C G D Am
1.
2.
na - ked and I'm far from
home. The
home.

26
D A/C♯ D/C G/B Gm/B♭ D/A C G
Save me, save me,
oh, I'm
na - ked and I'm far from

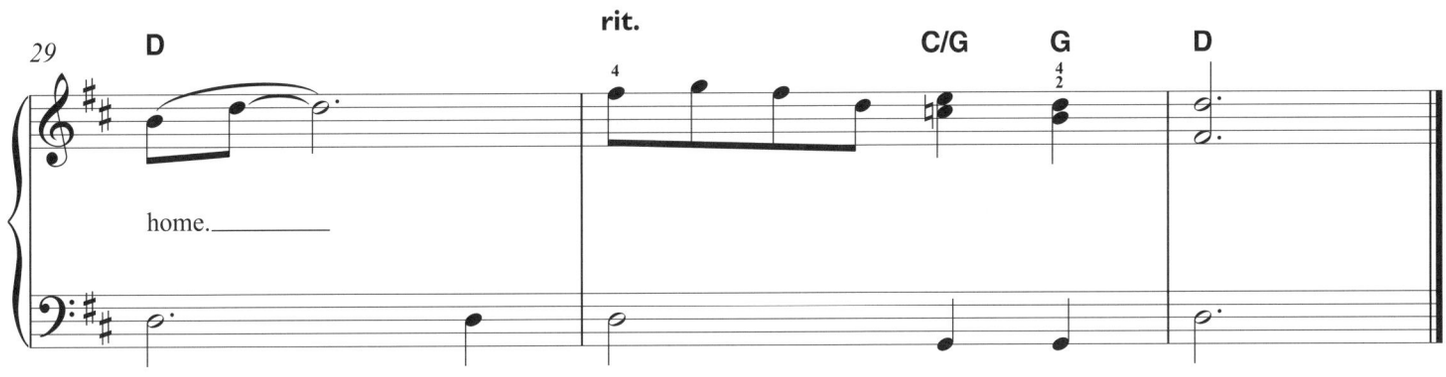
29
D
rit.
C/G G D
home.

Seven Seas Of Rhye

Words & Music by Freddie Mercury

Taken from their second album, *Queen II*, this song was rush-released following the band's appearance on *Top of the Pops* and in 1974 became their first major singles-chart hit. Inspired by a photo of Marlene Dietrich, the iconic monochromatic image of them on the LP's cover was echoed by it having a Side White and a Side Black.

Hints & Tips: Be careful of the accidentals from bar 14 onwards. Watch out for the high F♯ in bar 20; the long D in the bar before should give you plenty of time to make sure you land on the correct note!

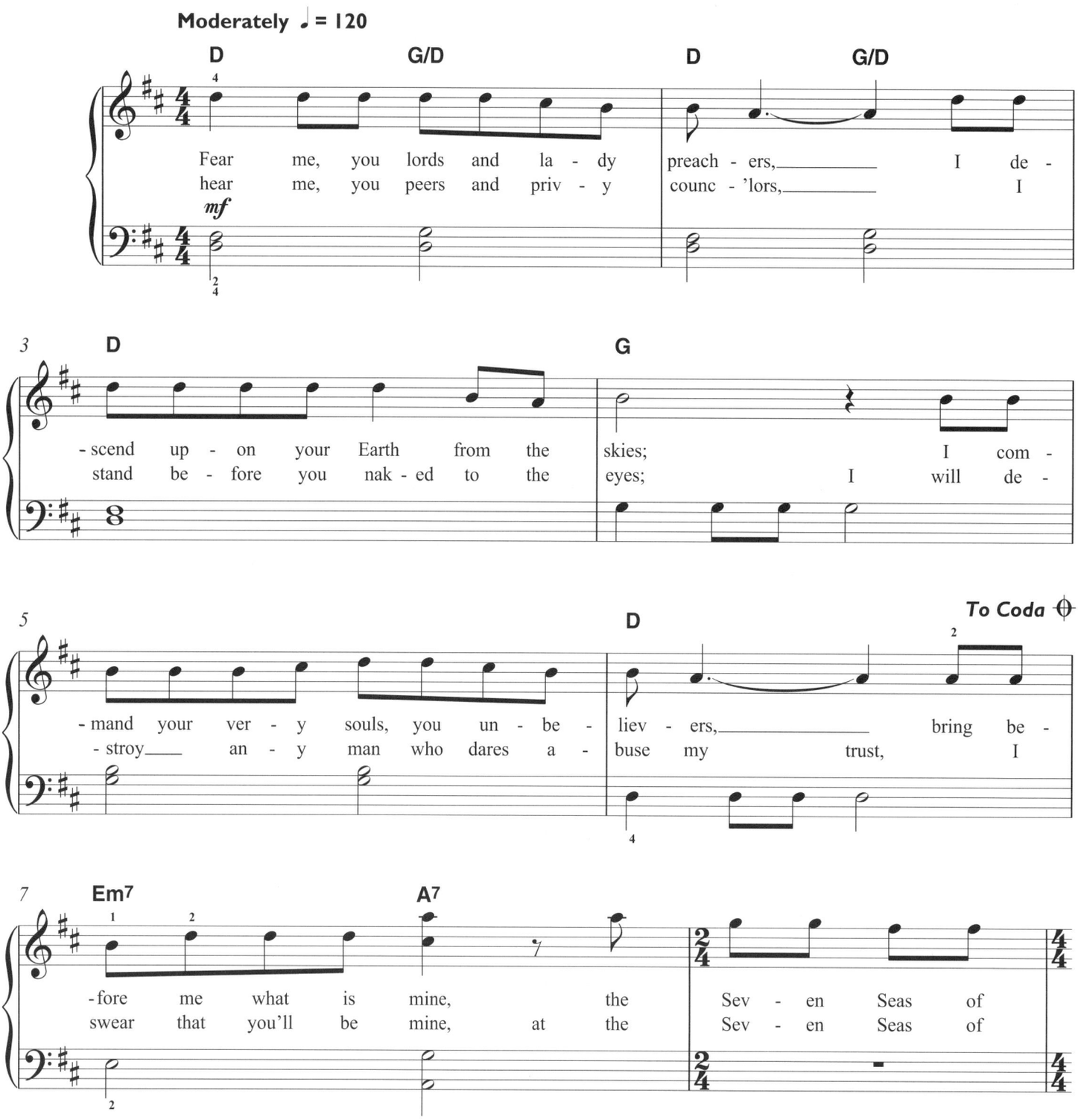

Copyright © 1973 Queen Music Ltd.
Copyright Renewed
All Rights Administered by Sony/ATV Music Publishing LLC, 424 Church Street, Suite 1200, Nashville, TN 37219
International Copyright Secured All Rights Reserved

1.
9
D
G
Rhye.
Can you
2.
11
G
D
C
G7
Rhye.
Sis - ter,
I live and lie for you,
14
D
C
G7
D
Em
Mis - ter,
do and I'll die;
you are mine, I pos - sess you, be -
17
D/F♯
G
- long to you for - ev - er,
19
Em
D
D
G/D
ah!

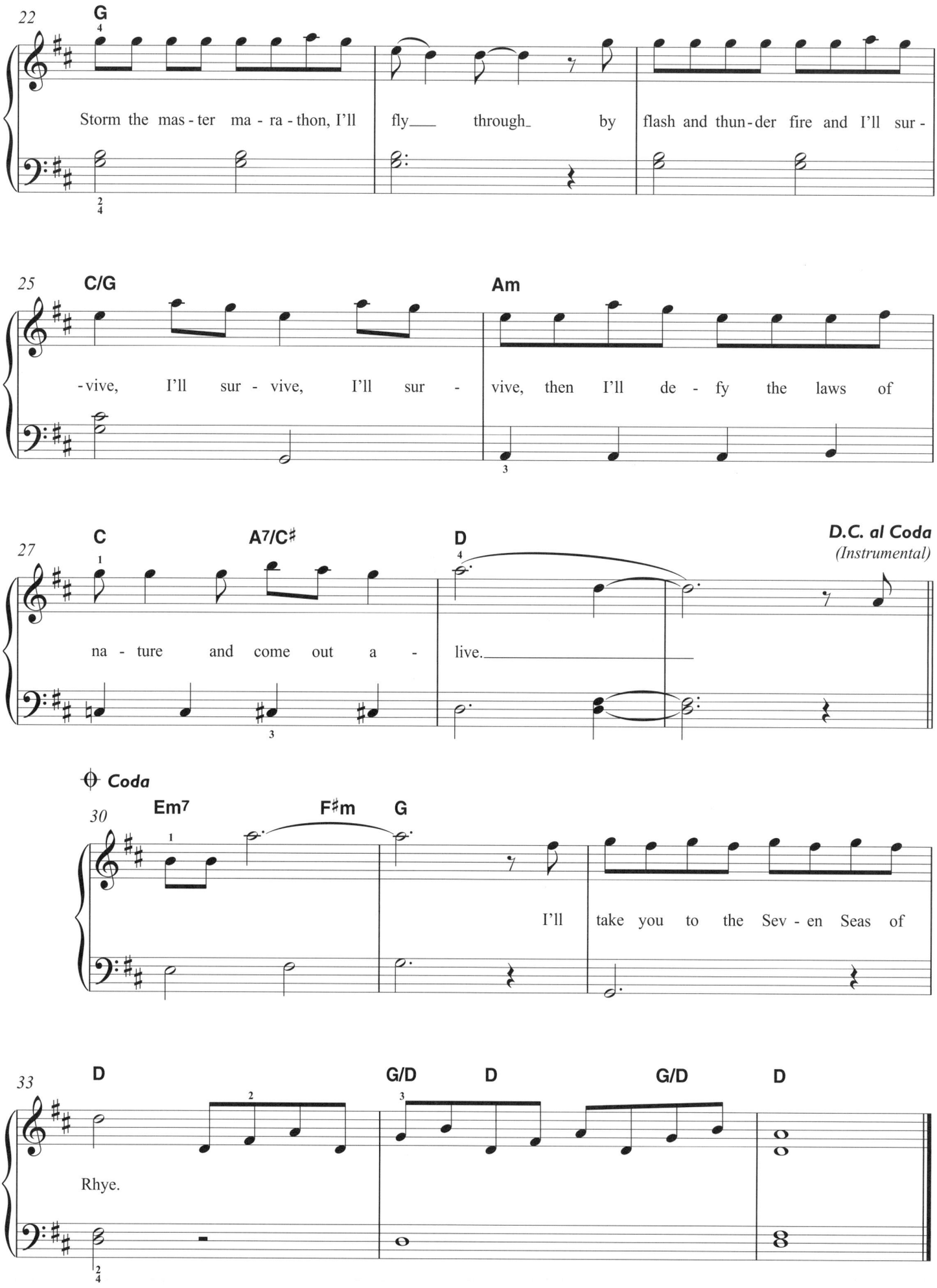
22
G
Storm the mas - ter ma - ra - thon, I'll fly through by flash and thun - der fire and I'll sur -
25
C/G
Am
- vive, I'll sur - vive, I'll sur - vive, then I'll de - fy the laws of
27
C
A7/C♯
D
D.C. al Coda
(Instrumental)
na - ture and come out a - live.
Coda
30
Em7
F♯m
G
I'll take you to the Sev - en Seas of
33
D
G/D
D
G/D
D
Rhye.

The Show Must Go On

Words & Music by Freddie Mercury, Brian May, Roger Taylor and John Deacon

Facing his impending death, although Freddie Mercury was too ill to make live appearances, he was not too ill to record and this song is about his continuing efforts to do so, despite his deteriorating health. Issued as a single in October 1991, it proved to be the last that Queen released before Freddie's death just six weeks later.

Hints & Tips: The right-hand eighth notes at the start should be played lightly, almost *staccato*. Go through the fingering of the melody so you know when to change your hand position.

Copyright © 1991 Queen Music Ltd.
All Rights Administered by Sony/ATV Music Publishing LLC, 424 Church Street, Suite 1200, Nashville, TN 37219
International Copyright Secured All Rights Reserved

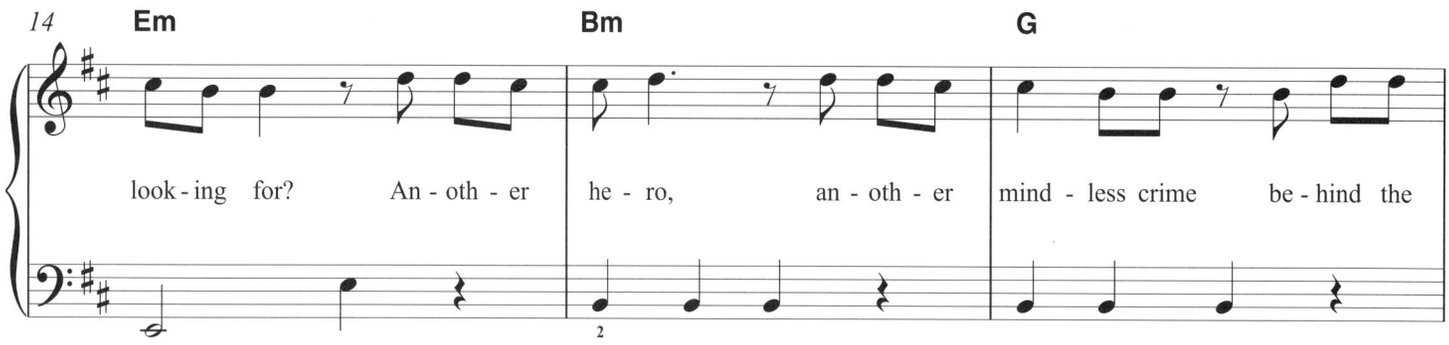
14
Em
Bm
G
look - ing for? An - oth - er he - ro, an - oth - er mind - less crime be - hind the

17
G
cur - tain in the pan - to - mime. Hold the line, does

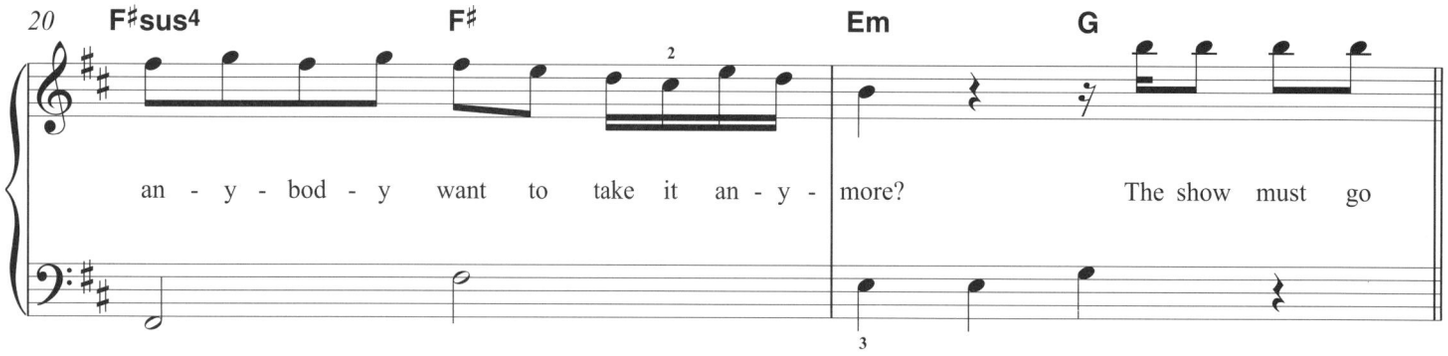
20
F♯sus4
F♯
Em
G
an - y - bod - y want to take it an - y - more? The show must go

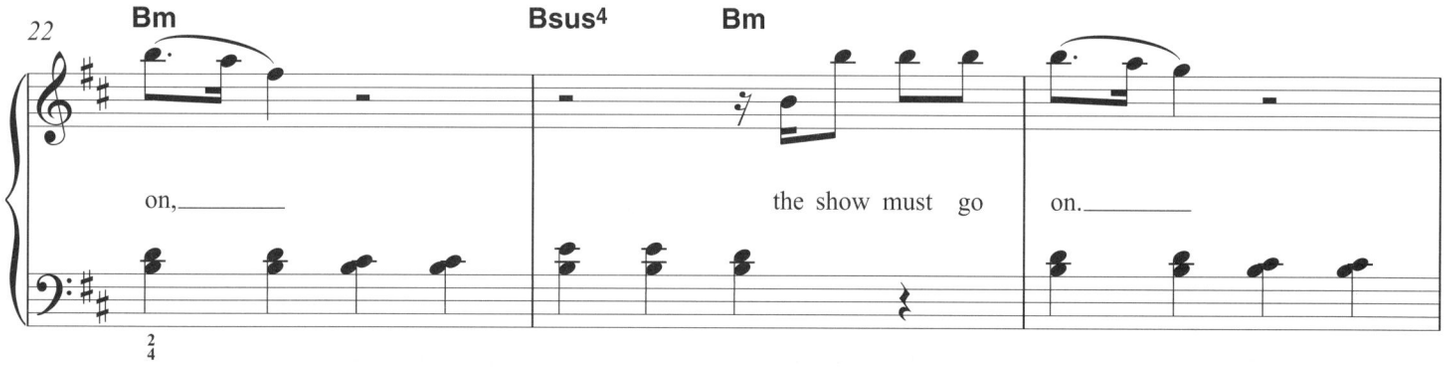
22
Bm
Bsus4
Bm
on, the show must go on.

25
Bsus4
Bm
Em
F♯sus4
F♯
In - side my heart is break - ing, my make - up may be flak - ing but my

28
Em
Bm
smile still stays on. The show must go on,

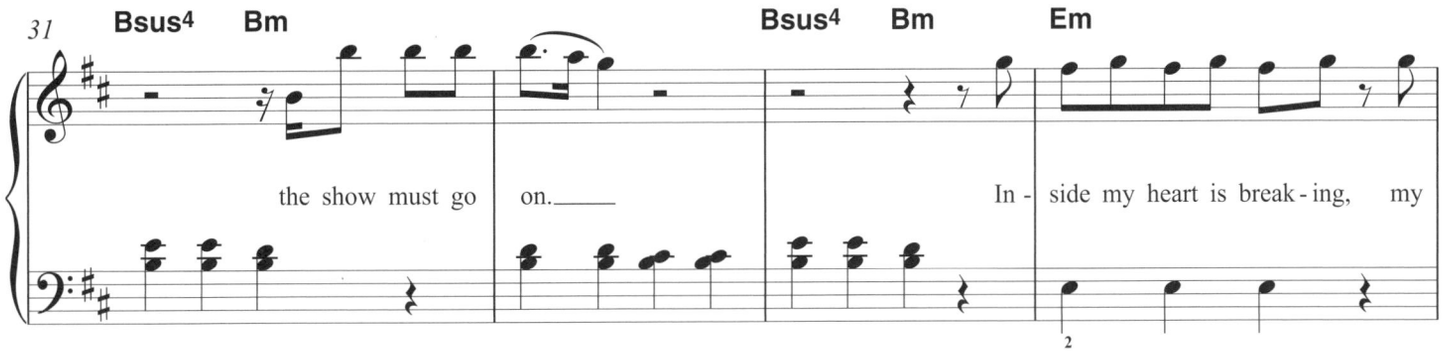
31
Bsus4
Bm
Bsus4
Bm
Em
the show must go on.
In - side my heart is break - ing, my

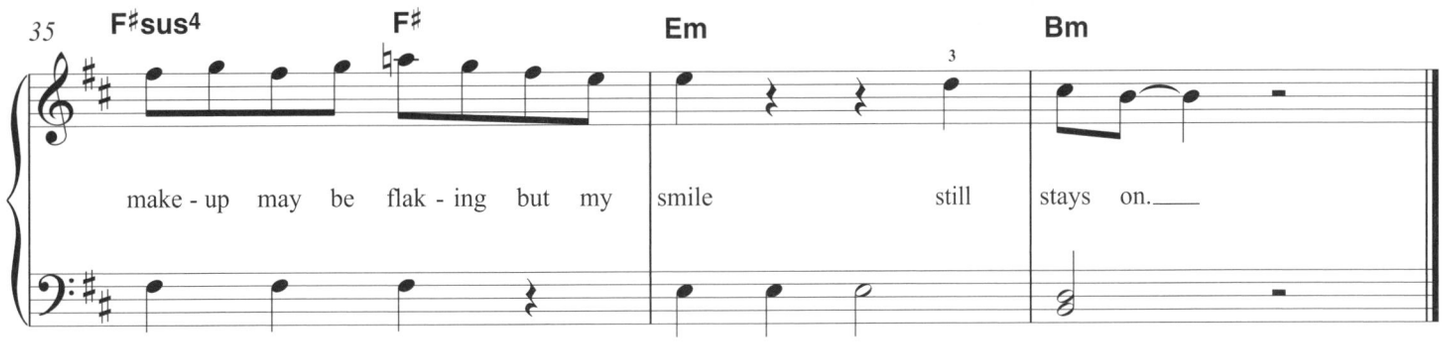
35
F♯sus4
F♯
Em
Bm
make - up may be flak - ing but my smile still stays on.

Somebody To Love

Words & Music by Freddie Mercury

The soul-searching lyrics of this song, the biggest-selling single from the album *A Day At The Races*, are about faith, with the singer questioning the lack of love in his life and the existence of God. The recording seemed to feature a large gospel choir, although layered vocal tracks enabled this to be achieved by just three voices.

Hints & Tips: Play through the right hand on its own a few times first until you're confident with it, as it's quite tricky in places. Note where the changes of time signature are so that the piece flows nicely all the way through.

Copyright © 1976 Queen Music Ltd.
Copyright Renewed
All Rights Administered by Sony/ATV Music Publishing LLC, 424 Church Street, Suite 1200, Nashville, TN 37219
International Copyright Secured All Rights Reserved

10
B♭ F/A Gm C7 F7
look in the mir - ror and cry: Lord, what you're do - ing to me? I have
12
B♭ C7 F C7/E F E♭
spent all my years in be - liev - ing you, but I just can't get no re - lief, Lord,
14
B♭ F/A Gm
some - bod - y, some - bod - y, can an - y - bod - y find me
16
B♭/F F B♭ F7 B♭ F/A Gm
some - bod - y to love? I work hard ev - 'ry day of my life,
18
B♭ C7 F B♭ Gm
I work 'til I ache my bones. At the end I take home my

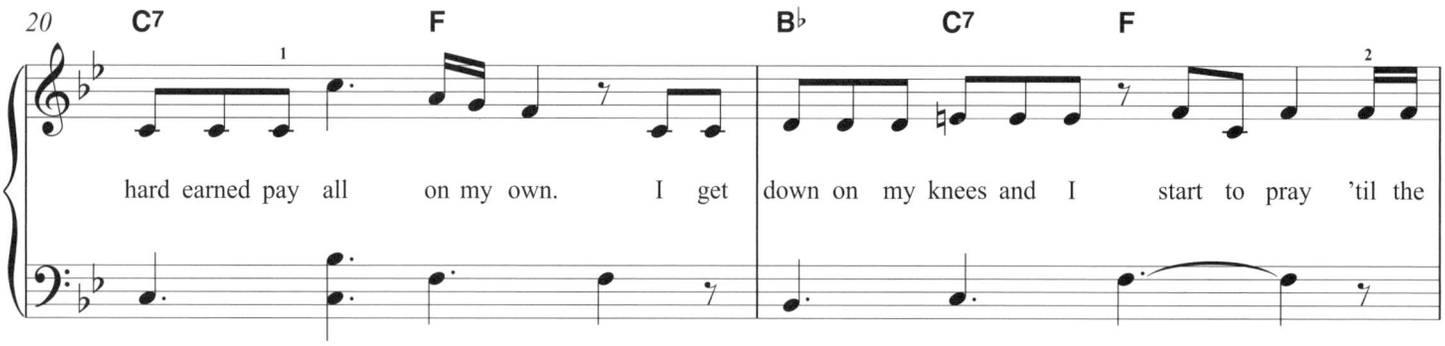
20
C7
F
B♭
C7
F
hard earned pay all on my own. I get down on my knees and I start to pray 'til the

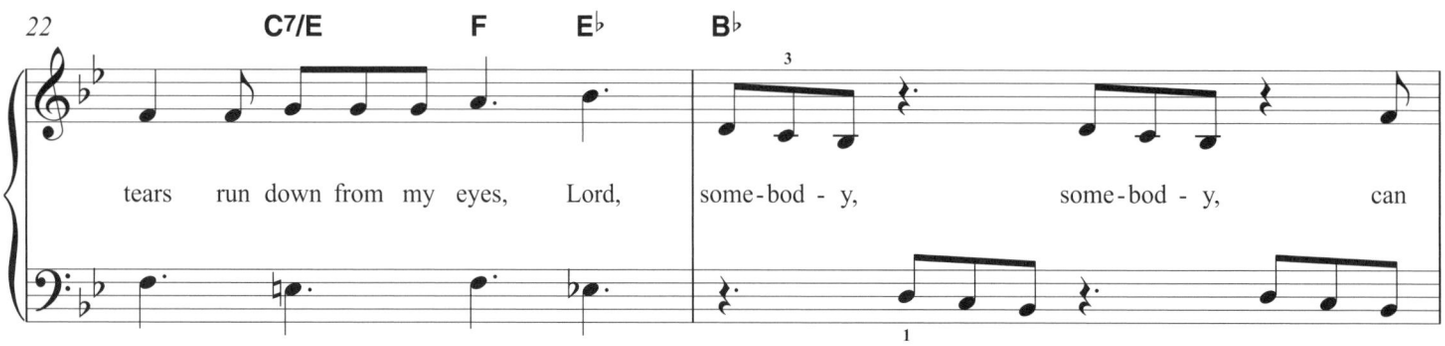
22
C7/E
F
E♭
B♭
tears run down from my eyes, Lord, some-bod - y, some-bod - y, can

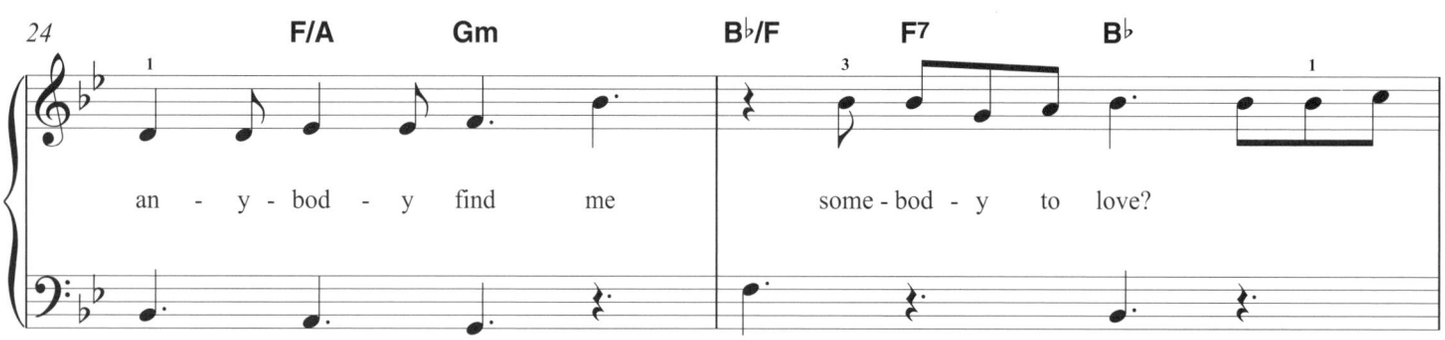
24
F/A
Gm
B♭/F
F7
B♭
an - y - bod - y find me some - bod - y to love?

26
F/A
Gm
E♭
rit.
F7
B♭

Too Much Love Will Kill You

Words & Music by Brian May, Elizabeth Lamers and Frank Musker

After Freddie Mercury's death in 1991, the remaining band members worked on a new project with the vocal recordings that he had left behind and in 1995 produced the album *Made In Heaven*, which features this song. Originally recorded as early as in 1988, it won the 1997 Novello Award for Best Song Musically and Lyrically.

Hints & Tips: Make the most of the melody in this; it should be played very expressively.

Copyright © 1993 Duck Productions Ltd., EMI Music Publishing Ltd. and Universal Music Publishing MGB Ltd.
All Rights on behalf of Duck Productions Ltd. and EMI Music Publishing Ltd. Administered by Sony/ATV Music Publishing LLC, 424 Church Street, Suite 1200, Nashville, TN 37219
All Rights on behalf of Universal Music Publishing MGB Ltd. in the U.S. and Canada Administered by Universal Music - Careers
International Copyright Secured All Rights Reserved

10
G
Em
G
me a - bout grow - ing up and what a strug - gle it would
shoes? Can't you see that it's im - pos - si - ble to
12
C
Am
Em
be. In my tan - gled state of mind I've been
choose. Oh, there's no mak - ing sense of it,
14
Am
Em
D
D7sus4
look - ing back to find where I went wrong.
ev - 'ry way I go I'm bound to lose.
17
G
C
Em
D
Too much love will kill you if you can't make up your mind.
Too much love will kill you just as sure as not at all.
mf
19
G
C
Em
D
Torn be - tween the lov - er and the love you leave be - hind. You're
Drain the pow-er that's in you, make you plead and scream and crawl. The

To Coda
21
G/B
G/D
C♯dim
head - ing for dis - as - ter 'cause you nev - er read the signs.
pain will make you cra - zy, you're the vic - tim of your crime.
23
G/D
D7sus4
G
Too much love will kill you ev - - ry time.
D.S. al Coda
25
C/E
G
C/E
D7sus4
I'm just the
Coda
28
G/D
D7sus4
G
Too much love will kill you in the end,
31
C
G
C
G
In the end.

Under Pressure

Words & Music by Freddie Mercury, John Deacon, Brian May, Roger Taylor and David Bowie

Memorable for John Deacon's distinctive bass line, this song came about from a collaboration between the band and David Bowie, who in 1981 was recording at the same studios in Montreux, Switzerland. They probably could not have imagined that their late night jam session would turn out to be an international No. 1 smash hit.

Hints & Tips: There are some tricky right-hand rhythms in this one; play the hands through separately until you've got the hang of them before trying hands together.

Copyright © 1981 EMI Music Publishing Ltd., Queen Music Ltd. and Tintoretto Music
All Rights on behalf of EMI Music Publishing Ltd. and Queen Music Ltd. Administered by Sony/ATV Music Publishing LLC, 424 Church Street, Suite 1200, Nashville, TN 37219
All Rights on behalf of Tintoretto Music Administered by RZO Music
International Copyright Secured All Rights Reserved

11
G/B
A
D
fam - 'ly in two, puts peo - ple on streets.
Boom, bah, bah, bay,
14
A/C♯
Bm
A
boom, bah, bah, bay, do, day, dah, do, day, dah, That's the
17
G
ter - ror of know - ing what this world is a - bout.
19
Watch - ing some good friends scream - ing, 'Let me out!' Pray to -
21
A/G
G
-mor - - row takes me high - - er; pres - sure

23
D/F♯
G
A
D
on peo - ple, peo-ple on streets.
Doo, doo, doo.
26
Ba, da, ba, ba, ba. O. K.
29
D
A/D
G/D
G/A
Chip-ping a - round, kick my brains on the floor. These are the days
32
D
A/C♯
it nev - er rains but it pours.
35
G/B
A
G/A
D

Who Wants To Live Forever

Words & Music by Brian May

Again, taken from the soundtrack of the film *Highlander*, set in the spectacular Scottish landscape, this song by Brian May frames poignant scenes in the film where Connor MacLeod cradles his dying wife Heather in his arms, realizing that, as an immortal who remains forever young, he will be without her for the rest of his time.

Hints & Tips: Take your time with this song — the tempo is marked *rubato*, meaning you can play the song at your preferred pace and add your own expression.

Copyright © 1986 Queen Music Ltd.
All Rights Administered by Sony/ATV Music Publishing LLC, 424 Church Street, Suite 1200, Nashville, TN 37219
International Copyright Secured All Rights Reserved

11
C
Bm
Am
wants to live for - ev - er?
wants to live for - ev - er?
1.
13
D7sus4
D7
Oh.
There's no
2.
15
Dsus4
D
G/B
C
Em
Oh.
But touch my tears with your
18
lips, touch my world with your fin - ger - tips. And
21
G
D/F♯
Em
G
D/F♯
we can have for - ev - er and we can love for -

24
Em
A/C♯
D
N.C.
-ev - er.
For - ev - er,
is
ours to - day.
27
B♭/D
G
D/F♯
Em
Who wants to live for - ev - er?
Who
30
G
D/F♯
Em
A/C♯
wants to live for - ev - er?
For - ev - er
is
33
D
B♭/D
rit.
ours to - day.
Who
36
Em
waits for - ev - er an - y - way?

We Are The Champions

Words & Music by Freddie Mercury

Of this anthemic power ballad, Freddie Mercury said: "I was thinking about football when I wrote it. I wanted a participation song, something the fans could latch on to." This certainly proved to be the case, as the song is still widely used to celebrate sporting victories and in 1994 was the official theme song for the *FIFA World Cup*.

Hints & Tips: Keep the left-hand arpeggios in the first half steady and flowing. Be aware of the key change in bar 18.

Copyright © 1977 Queen Music Ltd.
Copyright Renewed
All Rights Administered by Sony/ATV Music Publishing LLC, 424 Church Street, Suite 1200, Nashville, TN 37219
International Copyright Secured All Rights Reserved

16
C7
D7
G
mf
We
are the
19
Bm
Em
C
D7
G
cham - pions,
my
friends,
and
we'll
keep on
23
Bm
C
E/G♯
Am
fight - ing
to the
end.
We are the cham - pions,
28
Cm
F♯dim
G
F/A
Gm/B♭
we are the
champ - ions,
no time for
los - ers 'cause
we are the
33
C7
Dm
G
N.C.
Am7
G
1.
2.
rit.
champ - ions
of the
world. We are the
world.

We Will Rock You

Words & Music by Brian May

One of the most iconic Queen songs, 'We Will Rock You' was written by guitarist, Brian May, who had the intention of creating a song that could involve audience participation. It appears on their 1977 album, *News Of The World* and is followed by Freddie Mercury's track, 'We Are The Champions'. Because of this, the songs are usually played back to back — Queen would often end their live shows with both songs as a joint encore.

Hints & Tips: Keep the left hand steady throughout this song to maintain the pulsing, driving feel of the song. This song isn't too fast — be sure not to rush the right-hand sixteenth notes.

Copyright © 1977, 1978 Queen Music Ltd.
Copyright Renewed
All Rights Administered by Sony/ATV Music Publishing LLC, 424 Church Street, Suite 1200, Nashville, TN 37219
International Copyright Secured All Rights Reserved

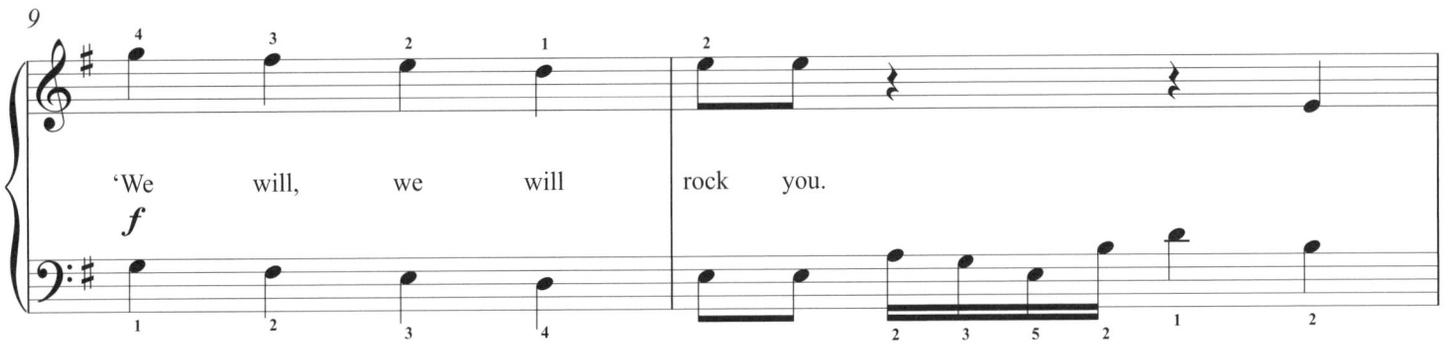
9
'We will, we will rock you.
f

11
We will, we will rock you.

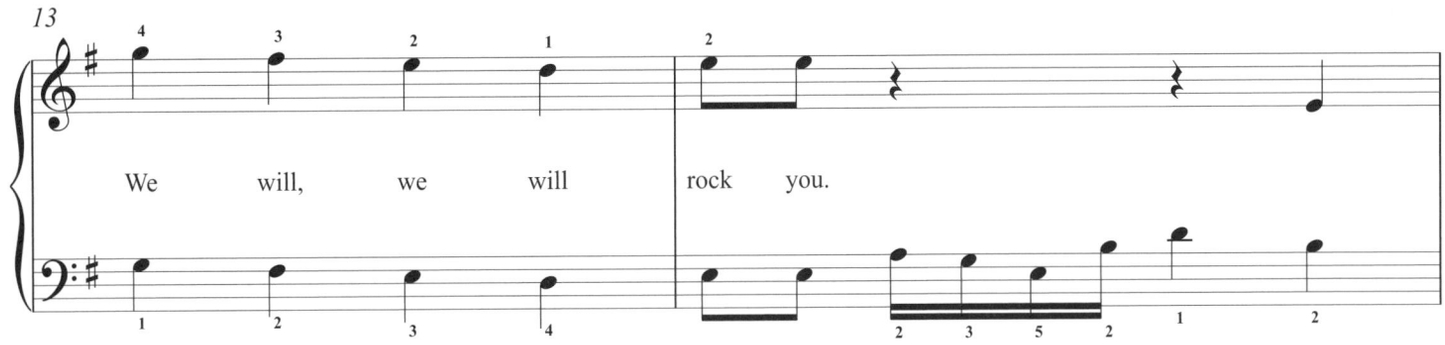
13
We will, we will rock you.

15
We will, we will rock you.'
ff

You're My Best Friend

Words & Music by John Deacon

Following on from Bohemian Rhapsody, this was the second single to be released from the 1975 album *A Night At The Opera*. The ballad was written by bass guitarist John Deacon for his wife Veronica, whom he had married in January of that year, and became a popular contrast to the band's more usual rock-orientated style.

Hints & Tips: This song has a swing feel. Use the quarter notes in the left hand to keep the beat steady and moving, but keep it light.

Copyright © 1975 Queen Music Ltd.
Copyright Renewed
All Rights Administered by Sony/ATV Music Publishing LLC, 424 Church Street, Suite 1200, Nashville, TN 37219
International Copyright Secured All Rights Reserved

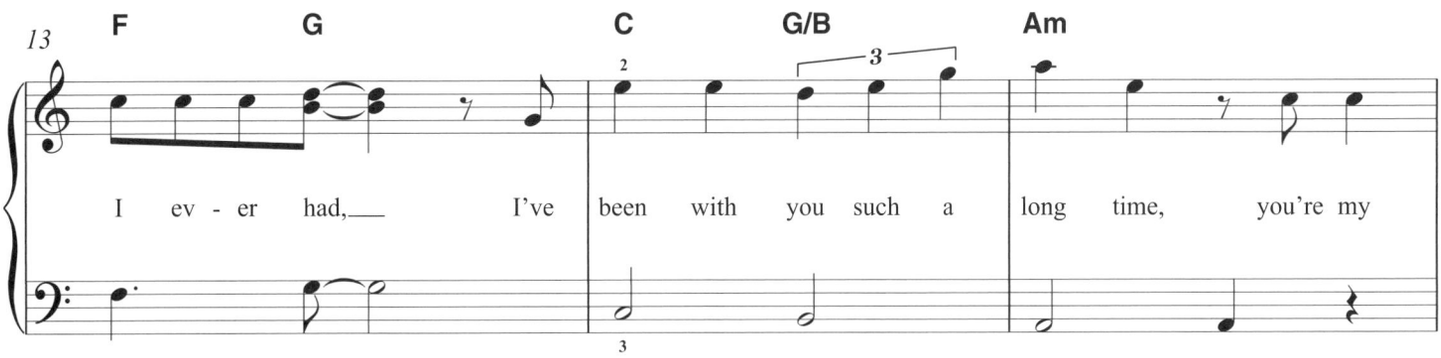
13
F G C G/B Am
I ev - er had, I've been with you such a long time, you're my

16
D F G E/G♯ Am
sun - shine, and I want you to know that my feel - ings are true. I

19
G F
real - ly love you. Oh, you're my

22
C
best friend.

24
Dm/C
C
E/G♯
Am
C/B♭
Ooh, you make me live.
Oh, I've been wan - der - ing 'round,

27
F/A
Fm
G
E/G♯
Am
D
And in rain or shine, you've stood by me, girl.
I'm

31
C/G
G
C
G C
hap - py at home.
You're my best friend.

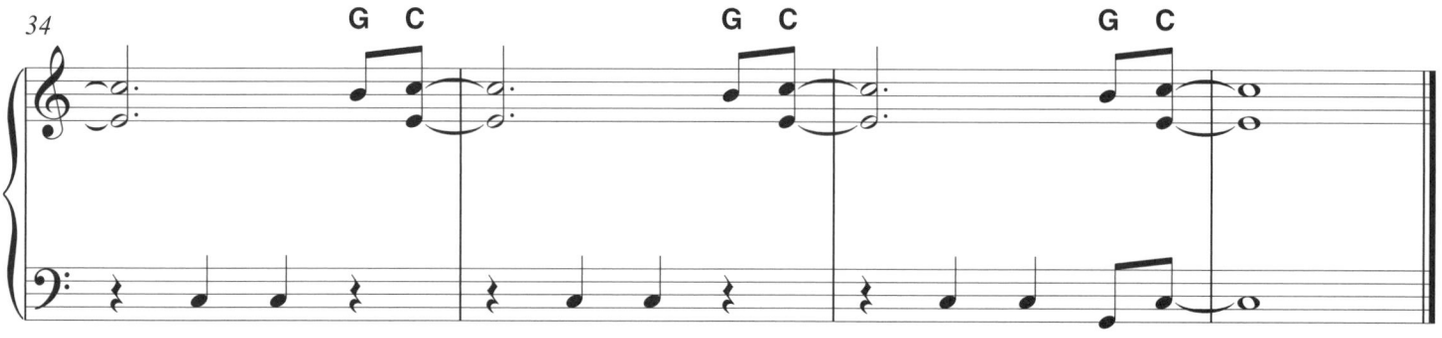
34
G C
G C
G C